12 Steps to
Reclaim your Power

*A self-help guide for women who are tired
of feeling stuck and settling for less*

Tanesia Harris, M.Ed., M.A.,C.P.L.C.

Dedication

I dedicate this book to God and my sun Eusiah Majesty. Dear Lord, you knew before giving birth to Eusiah, I was lost and confused, I didn't truly love, honor or respect myself. I believe you blessed me with a sun so I would have no choice but to embrace my light. Eusiah, because of you and God, I have made a commitment to love myself unconditionally. I know that you will learn more by what I do, rather than what I say. Therefore, I want to do all the things that God has called me to do so you can be encouraged to do the same. Me writing this book and publishing it, is just a start. Thank you both so much, I love you!

"For God has not given us a spirit of fear;
but of love, power, and sound mind."

2 Timothy 1:7

"Growth is painful. Change is painful. But nothing is as painful as staying stuck somewhere you don't belong."

-Mandy Hale

Contents

Introduction

Hello sweet lady! Thank you for taking time out to read this book. My name is Tanesia Harris and I am a Self-Discovery and Confidence Coach for Women. I believe, as women, we are natural born leaders. Our anatomy has been designed by the divine to create and teach who we know as society. We bring life into the world and hold the family together. It is our duty and responsibility to set an example for generations to come. In order to do so, we must love, respect, as well as, protect our mind, body, and soul. We are powerful beyond measure, and must understand that the vibrations we send out will radiate throughout everyone among us. That being said, phenomenal woman, I created this book to remind you how to live like the extraordinary D.I.V.A. you've been since birth.

In the following pages, I explain 12 ways you can reclaim your power that I have learned from my personal life, educational background, as well as my professional experience with psychology, coaching and counseling. I believe these steps are effective and can work for you, if you seriously put forth effort and time to practice them all.

While writing this book I kept in mind the fact that, these days very few of us have the time or attention span necessary to read long books. Between going to work, school, taking care of the kids if you have any, running errands, cooking, cleaning, etc., we get so tired that when we finally have a free moment we don't really feel like reading a book, especially for a long time. Not to mention with all the technology, latest gadgets and social media, it's hard for us to sit still and focus on one thing. We're living in an era where in one second with just one click you have access to so much information.

That being said, this book is short and sweet. It gets straight to the point as far as action steps you can take to get yourself out of a rut. As you read each step, I encourage you to fill in the blanks of how it applies to you and what you are currently going through in your life. You may find that some of the steps you have already taken while others you have not. For the steps you have not taken, may need to re-visit or feel confused about, more than likely they are the ones that have you feeling stuck. What's important is for you to recognize which steps have you feeling stuck and practice what each step suggests you can do to ultimately head in the direction where you would like to be. So without further ado, here they are.

1

Be Honest

e honest with yourself. Think about the situation that you are in and ask yourself how it makes you feel. When I say "it", it could be your job, a health issue/diagnosis, a romantic relationship, your living environment, your diet, your weight, your financial status, a caretaker role you are taking on, relationships you have with friends and family or the relationship you have with yourself.

If "it" makes you feel negative thoughts and emotions inside; furthermore, if "it" leaves you feeling overwhelmed, stuck and confused, then you have allowed "it" to take away your power. It's important for you to be clear about how people and situations are impacting your thoughts and feelings. If people and situations that you are affiliated with make you feel negative, then essentially you are surrounding yourself with negative energy.

Negative energy is unhealthy for your mind, body, and soul. The first step to change is awareness. Once you become aware that certain people and situations make you feel negative, for your personal growth and well-being, it's best to separate yourself from these people and situations. Don't allow the challenging circumstances you are experiencing to define who you are at the core of your being.

2

Set Boundaries

*I*t's not always so easy to remove yourself immediately from situations that produce feelings of discomfort and powerlessness for you, so you have to set up a plan of how you will be able to separate yourself; furthermore, seek assistance from third parties for support and reassurance that what you are doing is the best thing for you. It can be very scary and nerve wrecking to walk away from a job you hate or not satisfied with, but provides you with security, or a relationship with someone you love and have children with. It's not easy to stop spending time with family members and friends who are toxic, when you are used to spending time with them regularly throughout the year. It's very hard to eat healthy when you are always on the go and used to eating junk. Finding out you or someone you love has a disease or some form of disability can make you feel anxious or depressed and hopeless.

The reality is, you will more than likely feel lost and confused or nervous and lonely because letting go of the way you were used to living will be something completely new. It's important during this stage, to allow yourself to connect with people, places and things that remind you of why it's best to remove yourself from the unhealthy situation you're in.

This means that you will have to refer to people who have been through what you're currently going through and have overcome "it" or are coping with "it" in a healthy way, and, in addition, you may have to connect with a Therapist, a Life Coach, support group or trusted confidants to keep you feeling encouraged and supported as you put your well-being and personal growth first.

3

View Vulnerability as Strength

When connecting with people, it is important for you to speak your truth. Don't be afraid to let people know what you're thinking and feeling. Express your negative thoughts and emotions out loud, in this way, you release them from your insides. Walking away, setting boundaries and saying no to negative people and situations is just the beginning of reclaiming your power. To really be free from the negative energy that people and situations have produced within you, you have to let it all out. When I say "it", I mean the deep emotions that have you feeling stuck, scared, ashamed, guilty and embarrassed. Holding negative thoughts and emotions in, allows negative energy to build up within your body.

Negative energy can be very detrimental to your physical health because if you could just imagine for a moment, when your body is constantly tense, eventually it's not going to be so easy for your cells to function effectively. Your blood wants to flow freely, your cells want to be nourished and communicate with each other, in order to keep your body in homeostasis.

However, when you are filled with negative energy, this creates blockage in your body, so the cells and blood aren't going to flow so freely. You'll find that when you're really stressed, you may start to feel physically sick. For everyone, the symptoms and aches may be different. The key is releasing the tension and negativity, so your cells and blood can flow freely, hence, boosting your energy to get your body in motion, get you moving, taking action, rather than having you remain stagnant.

4

Develop Emotional Intelligence

*I*n order to express yourself and release the emotional blocks, you have to be clear on the emotions that you are experiencing and the thoughts that are running through your head. In order to communicate with others, you need the vocabulary and language to describe what is going on for you. Many of us know how to say I am happy or I am sad, but, not many of us have a huge list of emotion words we use to describe how we feel. If this is something you struggle with, you can google a list of emotion words, look up their definitions and pick which ones speak to whatever it is that you may be feeling. Additionally, you can buy books that talk about emotions in detail or connect with professionals like therapists, counselors or life coaches who specialize in managing emotions to help you understand your feelings.

It's important for you to really explore what you feel and where the feelings and thoughts you are feeling stem from. What caused you to think and feel the way you do? What do you believe is the reason why you think and feel the way you do? Where do these beliefs that you have stem from? Many times, we feel ashamed and embarrassed to admit that we are hurting or are in pain. We want everyone to feel like we've got it all together and we are invincible, but the truth is, we are human and flawed by nature.

No one is perfect or exempt from the inevitable trials life brings forth. "A closed mouth doesn't get fed." We have to be willing to admit that we are in pain, why we are in pain; furthermore, that we need help and support to overcome our pain. Don't allow your pride or ego to stop you from getting the help and support you need to rise above your adversity.

5

Identify Destructive patterns of Thoughts/ Behavior learned from your Upbringing and Environment

*M*any of us come from backgrounds where we are not used to talking about our feelings. We grew up in families where "children were seen and not heard." Being outspoken was considered a form of disrespect. Whenever there was conflict or any issues, instead of being addressed, they were swept under the rug. Everyone would move on as if everything was okay when in reality, none of the family problems were ever solved. As a result, now when you're going through things you may bear it all on your own or act like you're fine when you're really not.

Many of our thoughts and patterns of behavior stem from our family of origin or the environments in which we grew up. In order to examine your negative thoughts and beliefs, you have to identify negative life experiences, including, people and situations who currently or have previously caused you to develop discouraging thoughts and beliefs about your needs and capabilities. If you grew up in a home that was abusive, or you were rejected and neglected in your childhood, these kinds of situations can be devastating to your confidence and self-esteem. You may not feel very worthy or secure because people who were supposed to be loving and supportive to you, failed to meet your need for love, affection and belonging.

Experiencing racism, sexism or any form of abuse and oppression can negatively impact your self-esteem and confidence by making you feel inferior. Essentially these disgraceful acts can make you feel like, you aren't worthy of having your needs met. Abuse and oppression are demeaning and condescending. It's important to explore how such negative experiences can cause you to feel stuck and powerless. It's important to do so because if you don't take time to do so, you may find yourself repeating the destructive patterns of behavior you have been exposed to.

It's hard to be what you don't see. Therefore, we tend to stick to what we know. It feels uncomfortable when we step outside of our comfort zone. What I'm saying is, we need to be exposed to healthy relationships and treated with love and respect to break destructive patterns of thoughts and behavior passed on from our upbringing and environment. In this way, they aren't passed on to future generations. We have to be in tuned with ourselves to recognize when things are happening in our life that aren't aligned with who we are at the core of our being.

6

Develop Self-Awareness

*I*n order to know yourself or have self-awareness, you have to get clear about your skills, values and interests. You have to learn your strengths and weaknesses; you have to identify your needs. If you want to live in line with your purpose, then you have to know who you are and what you need. I believe that a lot of times we don't get what we want because we don't know what we want, and we don't know what we want because we are so busy allowing our time to be consumed by others, we allow other people's needs and interests to take precedence over our own. We have to explore where we learned that it was okay to sacrifice our needs to satisfy others.

A person who is self-aware knows how to separate their thoughts, beliefs, feelings and needs from the thoughts, beliefs, feelings and needs of others. In other words, when you are self-aware, you are clear on what you think and feel about yourself, different people, as well as, different situations. You aren't easily swayed by the perceptions of others because you take time to think about your feelings and thoughts to form your own beliefs. You are able to separate your perspective from the perspective of others.

Essentially, when you are self-aware you are able to embrace your individuality. Moreover, you know how to make decisions based upon what feels right for you, as opposed to what may be right for others. You are open to learning, but you use the knowledge and tools you receive to draw your own conclusions and guide your own path. In other words, you operate as a leader rather than a follower.

7

Gain Clarity of your Needs

What do you want or need that you haven't been getting? Psychologists suggest many of our behaviors and actions are motivated by our needs. We engage in different experiences and form relationships with different people as a way to satisfy our needs. We have physiological (i.e., food, water, sleep), safety, social, and psychological needs (Maslow, 1943). Everyone has 3 universal psychological needs; autonomy, relatedness and competence (Deci & Ryan, 2000).

We need to know that we can make decisions for ourselves, based upon our desires, rather than the desires of others. Basically we all want to feel a sense of independence. We don't want to have to depend on others for everything. We need to know that we can do some things for ourselves. We all need to know that we can use our skills to complete tasks successfully, as well as to adapt to our environment. So in other words, we need to know that we have the ability to survive regardless of whether or not our environment changes.

As far as relatedness is concerned, we all need to be in relationships where we are loved unconditionally and appreciated. We need to feel a sense of belonging where we are respected and acknowledged for our unique gifts (Deci & Ryan, 2000). Abraham Maslow, a famous psychologist, also suggested, we have a need for growth or to feel self-actualized. In other words, we need to reach our highest level of potential (Maslow, 1943).

Essentially, what I'm saying is, we need to be clear about all of our needs and surround ourselves with people and environments that help us satisfy our needs in a healthy fashion. Even though you may be aware of some of your needs, you may be allowing unhealthy people and situations to fulfill your needs. In addition, you may be trying to help people who you are incapable of satisfying their needs because you haven't satisfied such needs for yourself. "You can't give what you don't have."

8

Take Accountability & Responsibility for your Actions

*I*nstead of getting mad at people for what you're going through or blaming others for being in the situation that you are in, acknowledge that you have control over the way you react to the people or situations that have you currently feeling stuck. It's easy to say everything that is wrong with the people or the situations you are in, but it's kind of hard to really sit back and think about how and why you are allowing the people and situations to negatively impact you. The key word is allowing.

You can't control what people do or some situations that you are presented with in life, but you do have control over your reaction; you can control your response to the negative circumstances you are presented with in your life; you can control how you choose to think and feel about people and situations; and you can control your beliefs about what you experience. Choose to look at what you're experiencing from a positive perspective. What are you learning from what you are going through? How can the experience you are going through be good for your well-being and personal growth? What can you do if you are unhappy with what you are being presented? Consider what you can do more of, less of, start doing and stop doing.

9

Boost your Confidence and Self-Esteem

To promote your well-being and personal growth, it's important for you to recognize that you are worthy of having your needs met and you have a lot of skills and knowledge that can be useful to the world. You are capable of taking on tasks and successfully completing them. You can do anything you put your mind to that you are interested in or have been called by the divine to pursue.

"Where there is a will, there is a way." Don't just think about what you want to do in your head or talk about it with others, take action to bring your visions and goals into fruition. As you make goals and successfully complete them, you begin to feel better about yourself and your capabilities.

In order to practice using your skills and testing your abilities, you have to be active in the world. Take part in new experiences, meet new people and gain new opportunities that help to spark your creativity and boost your level of competence in different areas.

10

Stop Self-Sabotaging

When you are suffering and feeling pain, don't do things to hurt yourself, instead, heal your wounds in a positive way. Show yourself some love by indulging in self-care. Refuse to use or over indulge in vices like alcohol, drugs, cigarettes, unhealthy food or casual sex to escape feelings of pain, loneliness, discomfort, inadequacy, etc.

These types of behaviors are forms of self-sabotage. Self-sabotage is knowingly doing things that can ruin different aspects of your life and hinder you from reaching your highest potential. When you self-sabotage, you undermine yourself and act in ways that dishonor your mind, body and soul, and ultimately weaken you.

Self-sabotage and emotional blocks go hand in hand because if you are allowing yourself to remain in situations that threaten your health and well-being, and you aren't actively working on a plan to remove yourself from the toxicity, then something is blocking you from changing the quality of your life for the better.

Ultimately, what I'm saying is, face your negative feelings and explore where they are coming from. Allow your discomforting feelings to guide you to an understanding that change is necessary to adapt to different environments. Change allows you to overcome challenging situations you encounter throughout your life because it forces you to adjust and ultimately transform.

11

Replace Self-Sabotage with Self-Care

The opposite of self-sabotage is self-care. When you care about yourself, you are concerned about your well-being. You acknowledge and are aware of when you feel troubled, worried and anxious about your life. You are cautious about the things you do and involve yourself. You take heed and pay serious attention to your life and well-being. You are alert; you watch your back, and protect yourself from harm. You take a liking and fondness to yourself and show yourself love and affection.

Self-care is a conscious decision to be aware of, as well as satisfy your needs to make sure you remain in good condition. Self-care is looking out for yourself when you feel hurt or experience any type of maltreatment. Self-care is being concerned about your happiness. It's providing yourself with attention because to you it matters that you are okay. You want to make sure that you feel good, furthermore, that your mind, body and soul are free from dis-ease.

Self-care is the intentional act of taking time to ensure meeting your mental, physical, emotional, social, spiritual, romantic, and financial needs when your mind, body and soul indicates to you it is necessary. In other words, self-care is a deliberate, self-initiated decision to take time to satisfy yourself mentally, physically, spiritually, emotionally, socially, romantically and financially.

Do things to ensure good health for all aspects of your being; physically, mentally, emotionally, socially, spiritually, financially and romantically. Get a sufficient amount of rest each day, groom yourself, get your hair done, do your nails and eye brows, get a pedicure, take care of your skin, do facials and body scrubs. Pamper yourself, go to the spa and relax with a massage or foot reflexology. Exercise and eat mainly organic healthy plant based meals to keep your body/temple looking and feeling good. Speak your truth, release negative thoughts and emotions to others who are non-judgmental, supportive and trustworthy, write in a journal, blog, listen to music, spend time in nature or by water, for example, go to the beach or hiking in the mountains.

Book a hotel or go away for the weekend where you can bathe in a pool or soak in the Jacuzzi. Take a walk through the woods, allow yourself to breathe in fresh air. Take time out regularly to unwind and have healthy fun. Spend time with people you love that make you feel good. Set boundaries when necessary. Take breaks when you feel overwhelmed. Don't compare yourself to people on social media. Limit the time you spend online and watching tv.

Pray daily, read empowering scriptures from the bible, do yoga, meditate. Read to gain knowledge, take a class on something you find interesting, explore new places that spark your creativity and interests. Save money for a rainy day, put money to the side for self-care; spend more money on experiences rather than material goods. Take time to nurture your romantic life, go on dates, spend quality time with your love interest, cuddle, and explore your sexual interests with someone you're in a healthy, loyal committed relationship with or married to.

12

Control your Self-Talk

ven though it's great to have people you can turn to during times of distress, the reality is people won't always be available to comfort you when you need it. Therefore, when these times present themselves, you have to learn how to make yourself feel good inside on your own.

When you are down, pay attention to what you say to yourself in your mind, or in other words, be mindful of the thoughts that are running through your brain. Tell yourself, "I'M A THRIVER. I'M NOT GOING TO GIVE UP. EVEN IF I STARTED OUT AS A VICTIM, I WILL TRANSITION INTO A VICTOR." Declare positive affirmations, such as this one, or say empowering statements, uplifting quotes, and powerful scriptures out loud and in your mind to yourself daily. Sound is power, what we proclaim, we give life. As the scripture from proverbs in the bible suggests, "life and death is in the power of the tongue." What you say, you can actually speak into existence. In addition, you can attract situations to yourself based upon your thoughts.

Our thoughts impact our feelings and our feelings and thoughts impact our behavior. When you think positive, you feel good inside. When you think and feel good, you are able to behave in ways that bring forth your best self. You tap into the divine energy within you that is phenomenal. The divine energy is your soul. When you operate from your soul, the light within you and the essence of your being, you become powerful!

Conclusion

I n life, there will always be times when we feel overwhelmed and like what we are experiencing is too
much to bear, but you don't have to allow your
experiences to take away your soul. You can refer to the
12 steps to identify where you need to restore your power.
The 12 steps are a reference point to determine where
you feel stuck. The steps are a way for you to check-in with
yourself to uplift your mind, body and soul. Everything
starts with you. "We attract what we are," therefore what
shows up in your world is based upon what's going on for
you internally.

When you ignore your feelings and deny your needs,
you begin to lose your voice. You forget what you want,
how to stand up for yourself and end up settling for less
than you deserve or desire. If this sounds like you, you
need someone from the outside looking in to help you see
what you are missing. Ladies, "no woman is an island."
We all need cheerleaders and a strong support system
to help motivate and guide us, so we can grow through
changes in our lives. Unfortunately, we don't all have

family and friends who we can turn to for this kind of support. For those of you who lack such support, this is where a Life Coach like myself comes into play.

As someone who has been studying psychology and working in the helping field for over a decade, I am clear about how to help amazing women like yourself, who are exhausted from feeling stuck and settling for less, acquire what you truly desire, in your personal, professional and/or social life. I have used all the steps in my personal life and can provide you with the tools, knowledge and support you need to take each step. To learn more about me and the services I provide, email me @ gaincourage@gmail.com or visit www.InsightfullPerspective.com. Thank you so much for reading. Wishing you all the best and much success!

References

Deci, E.L., & Ryan, R.M. (2000).

    The what and why of goal pursuits; Human needs and the self determination of behavior. *Psychological Inquiry (11)*, 227-268. Retrieved from http://www.jstor.org/stable/1449618

Maslow A.H. (1943).

    A theory of human motivation. *Psychological review (50)*4, 370-396.

    Content is in the public domain.

About the Author

Tanesia Harris, M.Ed., M.A. is a Life Coach, Self-Help Author, and Motivational Speaker from the city that never sleeps. She helps women who are tired of feeling stuck and settling for less identify emotional blocks and self-sabotaging behavior holding them back from fulfilling their divine purpose.

No stranger to pain, Tanesia has had to navigate through challenging complexities in life, such as poverty, domestic abuse, single motherhood, co-dependency, as well as, depression and anxiety to name a few. After seeking God and professional help to heal/let go of pain from years of baggage and self-sabotage, Tanesia is now on a mission to help women who have been abused or come from dysfunctional families reclaim their power.

An Ivy League graduate, Tanesia holds a Master of Arts (M.A.) and Master of Education (M.Ed.) in Psychological Counseling from Teachers College, Columbia University. Additionally, she is certified as a Life Coach as well as a Circle of Security Parent Class Facilitator. To learn more about Tanesia, the services she provides and how she can help you or any women you know feel empowered to bring forth your best self, feel free to email her @ gaincourage@gmail.com or visit her website www.InsightfullPerspective.com.

Made in the USA
Middletown, DE
13 January 2022

58627634R00024